Conversational

Spanish

Dialogues

50 SPANISH CONVERSATIONS TO EASILY IMPROVE YOUR VOCABULARY & BECOME FLUENT FASTER

CONVERSATIONAL SPANISH DUAL LANGUAGE BOOKS VOL. 1

TOURI

https://touri.co

ISBN: 978-1-953149-19-0

Contents

Free Audiobooks 1

Resources 2

Free Spanish Video Course 4

Introduction 5

1. Saludo Formal – Formal Greeting 8

2. Saludo Informal – Informal Greeting 10

3. Una Llamada De Teléfono – A Telephone Call ...12

4. ¿Qué Hora Es? – What Time Is It? 14

5. ¿Puedes Decirlo De Nuevo? – Can You Say That Again? ...16

6. Coincidencias – Coincidences 18

7. El Clima – The Weather 20

8. Ordenar Comida – Ordering Food 22

9. Visitando Al Doctor – Visiting The Doctor 24

10. Pedir Direcciones – Asking For Directions.......26

11. Pedir Ayuda – Calling For Help 28

12. De Compras – Shopping 30

13. Haciendo Unos Mandados – Running Errands...32

14. En La Oficina De Correos – At The Post Office...34

15. El Examen – The Exam 36

16. El Suéter Perfecto – The Perfect Sweater 38

17. Taxi O Autobús – Taxi Or Bus 40

18. ¿Cuántos Años Tienes? – How Old Are You? ...42

19. En El Cine – At The Theater 44

20. ¿En Qué Eres Bueno? – What Are You Good At Doing?...46

21. ¿Cuál Es Tu Deporte Favorito? – What Is Your Favorite Sport?...48

22. Ir A Ver Un Musical – Going To See A Musical ...50

23. Ir De Vacaciones – Taking A Vacation 52

24. En La Tienda De Mascotas – At The Pet Store 54

25. Expresando Tu Opinion – Expressing Your Opinion 56

26. Pasatiempos – Hobbies...58

27. La Boda – The Wedding...60

28. Dar Consejos – Giving Advice..62

29. Enseñando A Niños – Teaching Children 64

30. Diversión Jugando Al Tenis – Fun With Tennis...........................67

31. Viviendo En California – Living In California 69

32. Horneando – Baking Goodness 73

33. Ayuda Por Teléfono – Help Over The Phone 77

34. Vamos A Un Concierto – Let's Go To A Concert 81

35. Haciendo Planes – Making Plans 85

36. Receso invernal – Winter Break 87

37. Visitar Al Doctor – Visiting The Doctor..91

38. El Mercado – The Market...95

39. Obtengamos Un Apartamento – Let's Get An Apartment 99

40. El Quiosco – The Concesssion Stand 103

41. El Almuerzo – Lunchtime 106

42. Buscando Trabajo – Searching For A Job 110

43. Entrevista de Trabajo – Job Interview 112

44. Dando Una Presentación – Giving A Presentation................116

45. Graduación – Graduation 118

46. Noche de Brujas – Halloween 120

47. En un Hotel – At a Hotel 122

48. Un Estudiante Extranjero – A Foreign Student.......................125

49. Procrastinación – Procrastination 127

50. Dónde Está Mi Hermano – Where's My Brother........................129

Conclusion 132

About the Author 133

Other Books By Touri 134

FREE AUDIOBOOKS

Touri has partnered with AudiobookRocket.com!

If you love audiobooks, here is your opportunity to get the NEWEST audiobooks completely FREE!

Thrillers, Fantasy, Young Adult, Kids, African-American Fiction, Women's Fiction, Sci-Fi, Comedy, Classics and many more genres!

Visit AudiobookRocket.com!

RESOURCES

TOURI.CO

Some of the best ways to become fluent in a new language is through repetition, memorization and conversation. If you'd like to practice your newly learned vocabulary, Touri offers live fun and immersive 1-on-1 online language lessons with native instructors at nearly anytime of the day. For more information go to Touri.co now.

FACEBOOK GROUP
Learn Spanish - Touri Language Learning

Learn French - Touri Language Learning

YOUTUBE
Touri Language Learning Channel

ANDROID APP
Learn Spanish App for Beginners

BOOKS

SPANISH

Spanish Short Stories (Volume 1): 10 Exciting Short Stories to Easily Learn Spanish & Improve Your Vocabulary

Spanish Short Stories (Volume 2): 10 Exciting Short Stories to Easily Learn Spanish & Improve Your Vocabulary

Intermediate Spanish Short Stories (Volume 1): 10 Amazing Short Tales to Learn Spanish & Quickly Grow Your Vocabulary the Fun Way!

Intermediate Spanish Short Stories (Volume 2): 10 Amazing Short Tales to Learn Spanish & Quickly Grow Your Vocabulary the Fun Way!

100 Days of Real World Spanish: Useful Words & Phrases for All Levels to Help You Become Fluent Faster

100 Day Medical Spanish Challenge: Daily List of Relevant Medical Spanish Words & Phrases to Help You Become Fluent

FRENCH

Conversational French Dialogues: 50 French Conversations and Short Stories

French Short Stories for Beginners (Volume 1): 10 Exciting Short Stories to Easily Learn French & Improve Your Vocabulary

French Short Stories for Beginners (Volume 2): 10 Exciting Short Stories to Easily Learn French & Improve Your Vocabulary

ITALIAN

Conversational Italian Dialogues: 50 Italian Conversations and Short Stories

FREE SPANISH VIDEO COURSE

200+ words and phrases in audio
you can start using today!
Get it while it's available

https://touri.co/freespanishvideocourse-spanish-dialogues/

INTRODUCTION

So you're ready to take the plunge and learn Spanish? What an excellent choice you have made to expand your horizons and open more doors to opportunities in your life.

If this is your first time or a continuation of your Spanish learning journey, we want you to know that we're proud of you.

Spanish is an incredibly beautiful language and spoken by nearly 500 million individuals around the world. As the native language of about 388 million individuals in 21 countries, including in Argentina, Spain, USA, Mexico, Colombia, Peru and Venezuela, it's easy to see why Spanish is the second most widely spoken in the world.

The ability to communicate in a foreign language will allow you to truly immerse yourself in different cultures, create even more memorable travel experiences and become more marketable for career opportunities.

It is human nature to naturally progress and learn from the day we are born. Since birth we have been shaping our preferences based on our previous experiences. These experiences have provided you important feedback about your likes, dislikes, what has made you better or worse and allowed you to learn from these lessons.

The same process should be taken to learn a language.

Our goal with this book is to provide engaging and fun learning material that is relevant and useful in the real Spanish-speaking world. Some students are provided with difficult or boring language materials that cause the learner to become overwhelmed and give up shortly after.

Building a strong foundation of vocabulary is critical to your improvement and reaching fluency. We *guarantee* you that this book is packed with vocabulary and phrases that you can start using today.

WHAT THIS BOOK IS ABOUT & HOW IT WORKS

A sure-fire way to exponentially decrease your time to Spanish fluency is to role play with key words and phrases that naturally occur in actual scenarios you experience on a daily basis.

This book has 50 examples of conversations, written in both Spanish and English so you never feel lost in translation, and will ensure you boost your conversational skills quickly.

You will find each chapter different from the last as two or more characters interact in real life scenarios. You will soon learn how to ask for directions, send a package at the post office, call for help, introduce yourself and even order at a restaurant.

Sometimes a direct translation does not make sense in to and from each language. Therefore, we recommend that you read each story in both languages to ensure understanding what is taking place.

TIPS FOR SUCCESS

No doubt you can pick up this book at anytime to reference a situation that you may be in. However, in order to get the most out of this book, there is an effective approach to yield the best results.

1. Role-play: Learning takes place when activities are engaging and memorable. Role-play is any speaking activity when you either put yourself into someone else's shoes, or when put yourself into an imaginary situation and act it out.

2. Look up vocab: At some points there may be a word or phrase that you don't understand and that's completely fine. As we mentioned before, some of the translations are not word-for-word in order for the conversations to remain realistic in each language. Therefore, we recommend that you look up anything that is not fully clear to you.

3. Create your own conversations: After going through all of the stories we invite you to create your own by modifying what you already read. Perhaps you order additional items while at a restaurant or maybe you have an entirely different conversation over the phone. Let your imagination run wild.

4. Seek out more dialogues: Don't let your learning stop here. We encourage you to practice in as many ways as possible. Referencing your newly learned phrases and vocabulary, you can test your comprehension with Spanish movies and television shows. Practice, practice, practice will give you the boost to fluency.

Focus on building your foundation of words and phrases commonly used in the real world and we promise your results will be staggering! Now, go out into the world, speak with confidence and in no time native speakers will be amazed by your Spanish speaking skills.

Good luck!

1. Saludo Formal – Formal Greeting

John: Buenos días, profesor Justin, ¿cómo está?

Profesor Justin: Buenos días, John. Estoy bien. ¿Y usted?

John: Estoy bien, gracias. Esta es mi amiga Clarissa. Ella está pensando entrar en esta universidad. Ella tiene algunas preguntas. ¿Le importaría contarnos sobre el proceso, por favor?

Profesor Justin: ¡Hola, Clarissa! Es un placer conocerte. Estoy más que feliz de hablar contigo. Por favor pasa por mi oficina la próxima semana.

Clarissa: Es un placer conocerle, profesor. Muchas gracias por ayudarnos.

Profesor Justin: Por supuesto. ¡Espero poder responder tus preguntas!

Formal Introduction

John: Good morning, Professor Justin, how are you doing?

Professor Justin: Good morning, John. I am doing well. And you?

John: I'm well, thank you. This is my friend Clarissa. She is thinking about applying to this university. She has a few questions. Would you mind telling us about the process, please?

Professor Justin: Hello, Clarissa! It's a pleasure to meet you. I'm more than happy to speak with you. Please stop by my office next week.

Clarissa: It's a pleasure to meet you, professor. Thank you so much for helping us.

Professor Justin: Of course. Hopefully, I will be able to answer your questions!

2. Saludo Informal – Informal Greeting

Jeff: ¿Quién es la mujer alta junto a Barbara?

Charles: Esa es su amiga Mary. ¿No la conociste en la fiesta de Steve?

Jeff: No, no estaba en la fiesta de Steve.

Charles: ¡Oh! Entonces déjame presentártela ahora. Mary, este es mi amigo Jeff.

Mary: Hola, Jeff. Encantada de conocerte.

Jeff: Yo también estoy encantado. ¿Quieres una bebida?

Mary: Claro, vamos a buscar una.

SALUDO INFORMAL

Jeff: Who's the tall woman next to Barbara?

Charles: That's her friend Mary. Didn't you meet her at Steve's party?

Jeff: No, I wasn't at Steve's party.

Charles: Oh! Then let me introduce you to her now. Mary, this is my friend Jeff.

Mary: Hi, Jeff. Nice to meet you.

Jeff: You, too. Would you like a drink?

Mary: Sure, let's go get one.

3. Una Llamada De Teléfono – A Telephone Call

John: Hola, Alice, soy John. ¿Cómo estás?

Alice: ¡Oh, hola, John! Justo estaba pensando en ti.

John: Oh que bueno. Me preguntaba si te gustaría ir al cine esta noche.

Alice: ¡Claro, me encantaría! ¿Cuál pelicula quieres ver?

John: Estaba pensando en la nueva comedia *Turn Off the Lights*. ¿Qué piensas?

Alice: ¡Suena genial!

John: Ok, te recogeré a las 7:30. La película comienza a las 8:00.

Alice: Nos vemos entonces. ¡Adiós!

A Telephone call

John: Hi, Alice, it's John. How are you?

Alice: Oh, hi, John! I was just thinking about you.

John: That's nice. I was wondering if you'd like to go to a movie tonight.

Alice: Sure, I'd love to! Which movie do you want to see?

John: I was thinking about that new comedy *Turn Off the Lights.* What do you think?

Alice: Sounds great!

John: Ok, I'll pick you up around 7:30. The movie starts at 8:00.

Alice: See you then. Bye!

4. ¿Qué Hora Es? – What Time Is It?

Natasha: ¿Qué hora es? ¡Vamos a llegar tarde!

Tony: Son las siete y cuarto. Estamos a tiempo. No entres en pánico.

Natasha: Pero pensé que teníamos que estar en el restaurante a las 7:30 para la fiesta sorpresa. Nunca lo lograremos con todo el tráfico de la noche.

Tony: Estoy seguro de que llegaremos a tiempo. La hora límite casi ha terminado. De todos modos, la fiesta comienza a las 8:00.

Pero sí necesito ayuda con la dirección. ¿Puedes llamar al restaurante y preguntarles dónde estacionamos el automóvil?

Natasha: Por supuesto.

WHAT TIME IS IT?

Natasha: What time is it? We're going to be late!

Tony: It's a quarter after seven. We're on time. Don't panic.

Natasha: But I thought we had to be at the restaurant by 7:30 for the surprise party. We'll never make it there with all this evening traffic.

Tony: I'm sure we will. Rush hour is almost over. Anyway, the party starts at 8:00.

But I do need help with directions. Can you call the restaurant and ask them where we park our car?

Natasha: Of course.

5. ¿PUEDES DECIRLO DE NUEVO? – CAN YOU SAY THAT AGAIN?

Luke: ¿Hola? Hola, Stephanie, ¿cómo van las cosas en la oficina?

Stephanie: ¡Hola, Luke! ¿Cómo estás? ¿Puedes detenerte y recoger papel extra para la impresora?

Luke: ¿Qué dijiste? ¿Puede repetir eso por favor? ¿Dijiste que recogiera tinta para la impresora? Lo siento, el teléfono se está cortando.

Stephanie: ¿Puedes oírme ahora? No. Necesito más papel de computadora.

Escucha, te mandaré un mensaje de texto diciéndote exactamente lo que necesito. Gracias, Luke. Hablaré contigo más tarde.

Luke: Gracias, Stephanie. Lo siento, mi teléfono tiene una mala recepción aquí.

Can You Say That Again?

Luke: Hello? Hi, Stephanie, how are things at the office?

Stephanie: Hi, Luke! How are you? Can you please stop at the store and pick up extra paper for the printer?

Luke: What did you say? Can you repeat that, please? Did you say to pick up ink for the printer? Sorry, the phone is cutting out.

Stephanie: Can you hear me now? No, I need more computer paper. Listen, I'll text you exactly what I need. Thanks, Luke.

Talk to you later.

Luke: Thanks, Stephanie. Sorry, my phone has really bad

reception here.

6. Coincidencias – Coincidences

Meg: Bueno, ¡hola, Julia! ¡Mucho tiempo sin verte!

Julia: ¡Meg! ¡Hola! ¡Qué casualidad! ¡No te he visto en años! ¿Qué estás haciendo aquí?

Meg: Acabo de conseguir un nuevo trabajo en la ciudad, así que estoy buscando algo de ropa. Oye, ¿qué piensas de esta camisa?

Julia: Emmm... bueno, sabes cuánto amo el azul. ¿Ves? ¡Tengo la misma camisa!

Meg: ¡ Siempre has tenido buen gusto! Qué mundo tan pequeño.

COINCIDENCES

Meg: Well, hello there, Julia! Long time no see!

Julia: Meg! Hi! What a coincidence! I haven't seen you in forever! What are you doing here?

Meg: I just got a new job in the city, so I'm shopping for some clothes. Hey, what do you think of this shirt?

Julia: Hmmm... Well, you know how much I love blue. See? I've got the same shirt!

Meg: You always did have good taste! What a small world.

7. El Clima – The Weather

Sally: ¡Hace mucho frío afuera! ¿Qué pasó con el informe meteorológico? Pensé que este frente frío pasaría.

Gabriela: Sí, yo también lo pensé. Eso es lo que leí en línea esta mañana.

Sally: Supongo que la sensación térmica realmente está bajando la temperatura.

Gabriela: ¿Podemos entrar? Siento que los dedos de mis pies comienzan a entumecerse.

The Weather

Sally: It's freezing outside! What happened to the weather report? I thought this cold front was supposed to pass.

Gabriela: Yeah, I thought so too. That's what I read online this morning.

Sally: I guess the wind chill is really driving down the temperature.

Gabriela: Can we go inside? I feel like my toes are starting to go numb.

8. Ordenar Comida – Ordering Food

Camarero: Hola, seré su camarero hoy. ¿Para iniciar puedo ofrecerles algo de beber?

Sean: Sí. Me gustaría té helado, por favor.

Anna: Y para mi limonada, por favor.

Camarero: Ok. ¿Están listos para pedir, o necesitan unos minutos?

Sean: Creo que estamos listos. Comenzaré con la sopa de tomate y la carne asada con puré de papas y guisantes.

Camarero: ¿Cómo quieres la carne, cruda, mediana o bien hecha?

Sean: Bien hecha, por favor.

Anna: Yo sólo quiero el pescado, con papas y una ensalada.

ORDERING FOOD

Waiter: Hello, I'll be your waiter today. Can I start you off with something to drink?

Sean: Yes. I would like iced tea, please.

Anna: And I'll have lemonade., please.

Waiter: Ok. Are you ready to order, or do you need a few minutes?

Sean: I think we're ready. I'll have the tomato soup to start, and the roast beef with mashed potatoes and peas.

Waiter: How do you want the beef — rare, medium, or well done?

Sean: Well done, please.

Anna: And I'll just have the fish, with potatoes and a salad.

9. Visitando Al Doctor – Visiting The Doctor

Doctor: ¿Cuál parece ser el problema?

Cathy: Bueno, tengo una tos fuerte y dolor de garganta. También tengo dolor de cabeza.

Doctor: ¿Cuánto tiempo ha tenido estos síntomas?

Cathy: Casi tres días. Y para ser honesto estoy realmente cansado, también.

Doctor: Hmm. Parece que tienes gripe. Hay que tomar aspirina cada cuatro horas y descansar mucho. Asegúrate de beber muchos líquidos. Llámame si todavia estás enferma la próxima semana.

Cathy: Ok, gracias.

Visiting The Doctor

Doctor: What seems to be the problem?

Cathy: Well... I have a bad cough and a sore throat. I also have a headache.

Doctor: How long have you had these symptoms?

Cathy: About three days now. And I'm really tired, too.

Doctor: Hmm. It sounds like you've got the flu. Take aspirin every four hours and get plenty of rest. Make sure you drink lots of fluids. Call me if you're still sick next week.

Cathy: Ok, thank you.

10. Pedir Direcciones – Asking For Directions

Marc: Disculpe. ¿Podría decirme dónde está la biblioteca?

Olivia: Sí, es por allí. Ve tres cuadras hasta Washington Street, luego gira a la derecha. Está en la esquina, frente al banco.

Marc: ¡Gracias! Solo llevo unos días en la ciudad, así que todavía no conozco mucho.

Olivia: Oh, sé cómo te sientes. Nos mudamos aquí hace un año, ¡y todavía no sé dónde está todo!

ASKING FOR DIRECTIONS

Marc: Excuse me. Could you tell me where the library is?

Olivia: Yes, it's that way. You go three blocks to Washington Street, then turn right. It's on the corner, across from the bank.

Marc: Thanks! I've only been in town a few days, so I really don't know my way around yet.

Olivia: Oh, I know how you feel. We moved here a year ago, and I still don't know where everything is!

11. Pedir Ayuda – Calling For Help

Peter: ¡Oye! ¡Ese auto se pasó la luz roja y chocó contra ese camión!

Gail: ¿Hay alguien herido?

Peter: No sé... llamemos al 911. ... ¿Hola? Me gustaría informar un accidente automovilístico cerca de la oficina de correos en Houston Street. Parece que un hombre está herido. Sí, acaba de suceder. Vale gracias. Adiós.

Gail: ¿Qué dijeron?

Peter: Van a enviar una ambulancia y un coche de policía de inmediato.

Gail: Bien, están aquí. Espero que el hombre esté bien.

Peter: Lo sé. Debes ser muy cuidadoso cuando conduces.

CALLING FOR HELP

Peter: Hey! That car just ran a red light and hit that truck!

Gail: Is anyone hurt?

Peter: I don't know... let's call 911. ...Hello? I'd like to report a car accident near the post office on Houston Street. It looks like a man is hurt. Yes, it just happened. Ok, thanks. Bye.

Gail: What did they say?

Peter: They're going to send an ambulance and a police car right away.

Gail: Good, they're here. I hope the man is alright.

Peter: I know. You have to be so careful when you're driving.

12. De Compras – Shopping

Louise: Oye Julia... ¡Mira a esos postres! ¿Qué te parece si horneamos algunas galletas hoy?

Julia: Hmm... Sí, ¡Es una gran idea! Mientras estamos aquí, recojamos los ingredientes.

Julia: Ok, ¿qué necesitamos?

Louise: La receta dice que necesitamos harina, azúcar y mantequilla. Ah, y también necesitamos huevos y chispas de chocolate.

Julia: ¿Por qué no compras los ingredientes lácteos? Los encontrarás en la sección refrigerada en la parte trasera de la tienda. Conseguiré los ingredientes secos, creo que están en el pasillo 10.

Louise: ¡Genial! Encontrémonos en la caja.

Julia: Ok. Te veo allí.

SHOPPING

Louise: Hey, Julia... Look at those desserts! How about baking some cookies today?

Julia: Hmm... Yeah, that's a great idea! While we're here, let's pick up the ingredients.

Julia: Ok, what do we need?

Louise: The recipe calls for flour, sugar and butter. Oh, and we also need eggs and chocolate chips.

Julia: Why don't you get the dairy ingredients? You'll find those in the refrigerated section in the back of the store. I'll get the dry ingredients. I believe they're in aisle 10.

Louise: Great! Let's meet at the checkout.

Julia: Ok. See you there.

13. Haciendo Unos Mandados – Running Errands

Recepcionista del hotel: Hola, ahi. ¿Como puedo ayudarte?

Claire: Bueno, estoy de visita por unos días, y necesito hacer algunas cosas mientras estoy aquí.

Recepcionista del hotel: Claro. ¿Que necesitas?

Claire: Necesito cortarme el pelo. También necesito que mis nuevos pantalones estén doblados.

Recepcionista del hotel: Ok. Aquí hay un mapa de la ciudad. Hay una buena peluquería aquí, que está a solo una cuadra de distancia. Y hay un sastre aquí mismo. ¿Hay algo mas?

Claire: Sí. ¡Tendré que hacer reparar el automóvil antes de mi larga vuelta a casa!

Recepcionista del hotel: No hay problema. Hay un buen mecánico a unas pocas cuadras.

RUNNING ERRANDS

Hotel receptionist: Hello there. How can I help you?

Claire: Well, I'm in town visiting for a few days, and I need to get some things done while I'm here.

Hotel receptionist: Sure. What do you need?

Claire: I need to get my hair cut. I also need to have my new pants hemmed.

Hotel receptionist: Ok. Here's a map of the city. There's a good hair salon here, which is just a block away. And there's a tailor right here. Is there anything else?

Claire: Yes. I'll need to get my car serviced before my long drive back home!

Hotel receptionist: No problem. There's a good mechanic a few blocks away.

14. En La Oficina De Correos – At The Post Office

Secretario postal: ¿Cómo puedo ayudarlo hoy?

Carol: Necesito enviar este paquete por correo a Nueva York, por favor.

Secretario postal: Bien, veamos cuánto pesa … son alrededor de cinco libras. Si lo envía expreso, llegará allí mañana. O puede enviar prioridad y llegará el sábado.

Carol: El sábado está bien. ¿Cuánto será eso?

Secretario postal: $12.41. ¿Necesita algo más?

Carol: ¡Oh, sí! Casi lo olvidé. Necesito un libro de sellos de correos, también.

Secretario postal: Ok, su total asciende a $18.94.

AT THE POST OFFICE

Postal clerk: What can I help you today?

Carol: I need to mail this package to New York, please.

Postal clerk: Ok, let's see how much it weighs... it's about five pounds. If you send it express, it will get there tomorrow. Or you can send it priority and it will get there by Saturday.

Carol: Saturday is fine. How much will that be?

Postal clerk: $12.41. Do you need anything else?

Carol: Oh, yeah! I almost forgot. I need a book of stamps, too.

Postal clerk: Ok, your total comes to $18.94.

15. El Examen – The Exam

Cheryl: ¡Hola! ¿Cómo fue tu examen de física?

FRANK: No fue mal, gracias. ¡Me alegro de que se haya terminado! ¿Qué tal tu... cómo fue tu presentación ?

Cheryl: Oh, fue realmente bien. ¡Gracias por ayudarme con eso!

Frank: No hay problema. Entonces ... ¿tienes ganas de estudiar mañana para nuestro examen de matemáticas?

Cheryl: Sí, claro! Ven a mi casa a las 10:00 am, después del desayuno.

Frank: Está bien. Traeré mis apuntes.

Catching Up

Cheryl: Hey! How did your physics exam go?

Frank: Not bad, thanks. I'm just glad it's over! How about your... how'd your presentation go?

Cheryl: Oh, it went really well. Thanks for helping me with it!

Frank: No problem. So... do you feel like studying tomorrow for our math exam?

Cheryl: Yeah, sure! Come over around 10:00 am, after breakfast.

Frank: All right. I'll bring my notes.

16. El Suéter Perfecto – The Perfect Sweater

Vendedor: ¿Puedo ayudarla?

Gloria: Sí, estoy buscando un suéter, en una talla mediana.

Vendedor: Veamos ... aquí hay uno blanco y bonito. ¿Qué piensas?

Gloria: Creo que preferiría tenerlo en azul.

Vendedor: Ok ... aquí está el azul, en talla mediana. ¿Te gustaría probarlo?

Gloria: Ok ... sí, me encanta. Queda perfecto. ¿Cuánto cuesta?

Vendedor: Son $41. Será $50, con impuestos.

Gloria: ¡Perfecto! Me lo llevo. Gracias!

THE PERFECT SWEATER

Salesperson: Can I help you?

Gloria: Yes, I'm looking for a sweater — in a size medium.

Salesperson: Let's see... here's a nice white one. What do you think?

Gloria: I think I'd rather have it in blue.

Salesperson: Ok ... here's blue, in a medium. Would you

like to try it on?

Gloria: Ok ... yes, I love it. It fits perfectly. How much is it?

Salesperson: It's $41. It will be $50, with tax.

Gloria: Perfect! I'll take it. Thank you!

17. Taxi o Autobús – Taxi Or Bus

Joyce: ¿Deberíamos tomar un taxi o un bus para ir al cine?

Bill: Tomemos un bus. Es imposible obtener un taxi durante la hora punta.

Joyce: ¿No es esa una parada de buses?

Bill: Sí... ¡Oh! Allí hay uno. Tendremos que correr para poder subirnos.

Joyce: ¡Oh, no! Nos perdimos el bus.

Bill: No hay problema. Llegará otro en 10 minutos.

TAXI OR BUS

Joyce: Should we take a taxi or a bus to the movie theater?

Bill: Let's take a bus. It's impossible to get a taxi during rush hour.

Joyce: Isn't that a bus stop over there?

Bill: Yes... Oh! There's a bus now. We'll have to run to catch it.

Joyce: Oh, no! We just missed it.

Bill: No problem. There'll be another one in 10 minutes.

18. ¿Cuántos Años Tienes? – How Old Are You?

Gloria: ¡Estoy muy emocionado por la fiesta sorpresa de cumpleaños de la tía Mary esta tarde! ¿Y tú?

Nadia: ¡Sí! ¿Qué edad tiene ella?

Gloria: Tendrá 55 años el 5 de mayo.

Nadia: ¡Guau! No sabía que mi madre era mayor: tendrá 58 años el 9 de octubre. De todos modos, ¡la tía Mary estará tan sorprendida de vernos a todos aquí!

Gloria: ¡Lo sé! Pero aún tenemos que preparar toda la comida antes de que llegue aquí ... ¡Está bien! Estamos todos listos ahora. Shh! ¡Ella está aquí!

Todo: ¡Sorpresa!

HOW OLD ARE YOU?

Gloria: I'm really excited for Aunt Mary's surprise birthday party this afternoon! Aren't you?

Nadia: Yeah! How old is she?

Gloria: She'll be 55 on May 5.

Nadia: Wow! I didn't know that my mom was older — she's going to be 58 on October 9. Anyway, Aunt Mary's going to be so surprised to see us all here!

Gloria: I know! But we still have to get all the food set up before she gets here ... Ok! We're all ready now. Shh! She's here!

All: Surprise!

19. En El Cine – At The Theater

Bob: Queremos dos boletos para el espectáculo a las 3:30, por favor.

Venta de boletos: Aquí tienes. ¡Disfruta la pelicula!

[Dentro del teatro]

Bob: ¿Te importaría cambiarte de asiento, para que mi amigo y yo podamos sentarnos juntos?

Mujer: No, claro que no.

Bob: ¡Muchas gracias!

AT THE THEATER

Bob: We'd like two tickets for the 3:30 show, please.

Ticket sales: Here you go. Enjoy the movie!

[Inside the theater]

Bob: Would you mind moving over one, so my friend and I can sit together?

Woman: No, not at all.

Bob: Thank you so much!

20. ¿En Qué Eres Bueno? – What Are You Good At Doing?

Sandra: Entonces ... ¿qué deberíamos hacer?

Julie: Bueno, me gusta hacer manualidades, y soy muy buena en dibujo. ¿Qué piensas?

Sandra: Hmm ... ¿qué tal jugar un juego de mesa? Eso sería más divertido.

Julie: Ok. ¡Juguemos al Scrabble! ¡También soy muy buena para deletrear!

Sandra: Oh, ¿sí? ¡Ya lo veremos!

WHAT ARE YOU GOOD AT DOING?

Sandra: So ... what should we do?

Julie: Well, I like to do arts and crafts, and I'm really good at drawing. What do you think?

Sandra: Hmm ... how about playing a board game? That would be more fun.

Julie: Ok. Let's play Scrabble! I'm really good at spelling, too!

Sandra: Oh, yeah? We'll see about that!

21. ¿Cuál Es Tu Deporte Favorito? – What Is Your Favorite Sport?

Phil: ¿A qué hora es ese partido de fútbol? Pensé que comenzó al mediodía.

Jack: Debimos haber tenido la hora incorrecta. Ah, bueno... el fútbol no es mi deporte favorito de todos modos. Yo prefiero el baloncesto.

Phil: Oh, ¿en serio? ¡Pensé que tu deporte favorito era el tenis! También soy un gran fanático del baloncesto.

Jack: ¿Qué tal si jugamos?

Phil: ¡Claro! ¿Por qué no vamos a lanzar algunos balones ahora ya que el juego de fútbol no está todavia?

Jack: Excelente idea. Vámonos.

WHAT IS YOUR FAVORITE SPORT?

Phil: What time is that soccer game on? I thought it started at noon.

Jack: We must have had the wrong time. Oh, well ... soccer's not my favorite sport anyway. I much prefer basketball.

Phil: Oh, really? I thought your favorite sport was tennis! I'm a big fan of basketball, too.

Jack: How about a game sometime?

Phil: Sure thing! Why don't we go shoot some hoops now since the soccer game isn't on?

Jack: Excellent idea. Let's go.

22. Ir A Ver Un Musical – Going To See A Musical

Shannon: ¡Qué actuación tan fantástica! Gracias por invitarme al musical.

Elena: De nada. Estoy feliz de que hayas disfrutado el espectáculo. La coreografía de los bailarines fue increíble. Me recuerda cuando solía bailar hace muchos años.

Shannon: ¡Lo sé! Fuiste una bailarina tan talentosa. ¿Echas de menos bailar?

Elena: Oh, eso es muy amable de tu parte, Shannon. Lo extraño a veces pero siempre seré fanática de las artes. Es por eso que me encanta ir a los musicales porque es la combinación perfecta de baile, canción y teatro.

Shannon: ¡Por supuesto! Me alegra que todavía seas una fanática del arte también. Gracias por la invitación. Siempre es un placer asistir a un evento artístico contigo y aprender algo nuevo.

GOING TO SEE A MUSICAL

Shannon: What a fantastic performance! Thank you for inviting me to the musical.

Elena: You are welcome. I'm happy you enjoyed the show. The choreography of the dancers was incredible. It reminds me of when I used to dance many years ago.

Shannon: I know! You were such a talented ballerina. Do you miss dancing?

Elena: Oh, that's very kind of you, Shannon. I do miss it sometimes. But I will always be a fan of the arts. That's why I love going to musicals because it's the perfect combination of dance, song and theater.

Shannon: Absolutely! I'm glad you are still an art fan too. Thank you for the invitation. It's always a pleasure to attend an arts event with you and learn something new.

23. Ir De Vacaciones – Taking A Vacation

Julie: Acabo de comprar un boleto a la ciudad de Nueva York. ¡Estoy tan emocionado de ver la ciudad!

Sophie: ¡Bien por ti! Viajar es muy divertido. Me encanta descubrir nuevos lugares y nuevas personas. ¿Cuando te vas?

Julie: La próxima semana. Estoy tomando el vuelo nocturno. Fue más barato. Con suerte, podré dormir en el avión.

Sophie: ¡Ojalá pudiera ir contigo! La ciudad de Nueva York es un lugar mágico. Te divertirás mucho.

Julie: Eso espero. Voy a visitar a mi hermano que vive allí. Me quedaré por una semana y luego tomaré el tren a Washington, DC.

Sophie: Eso suena fantástico. Tengo muchas ganas de pasar una semana en la playa para mis vacaciones de verano. Solo quiero relajarme.

TAKING A VACATION

Julie: I just bought a ticket to New York City. I'm so excited to see the city!

Sophie: Good for you! Traveling is so much fun. I love discovering new places and new people. When are you leaving?

Julie: Next week. I'm taking the red eye. It was cheaper.

Hopefully, I'll be able to sleep on the plane.

Sophie: I wish I could go with you! New York City is a magical place. You will have so much fun.

Julie: I hope so. I'm going to visit my brother who lives there. I will stay for a week and then take the train down to Washington, DC

Sophie: That sounds like a great vacation. I'm looking forward to a week at the beach for my summer vacation. I just want to relax.

24. En La Tienda De Mascotas – At The Pet Store

Connie: ¡Que gato tan hermoso! ¿Qué piensas?

Gary: Creo que preferiría tener un perro. Los perros son más leales que los gatos. Los gatos son perezosos.

Connie: Sí, ¡pero ellos necesitan mucha atención! ¿Estaría dispuesto a caminar todos los días? ¿Y limpiar después?

Gary: Hmm. Buen punto. ¿Qué hay de un pájaro? ¿O un pez?

Connie: Tendríamos que invertir mucho dinero en una jaula o una pecera. ¡Y honestamente no sé cuidar a un pájaro o un pez!

Gary: Bueno, obviamente no estamos listos para tener una mascota todavía.

Connie: Jaja... Sí, tienes razón. Vamos a comer algo y hablar de eso.

AT THE PET STORE

Connie: What a beautiful cat! What do you think?

Gary: I think I'd rather get a dog. Dogs are more loyal than cats. Cats are just lazy.

Connie: Yes, but they need so much attention! Would you be willing to walk it every single day? And clean up after it?

Gary: Hmm. Good point. What about a bird? Or a fish?

Connie: We'd have to invest a lot of money in a cage or a fish tank. And I honestly don't know how to take care of a bird or a fish!

Gary: Well, we're obviously not ready to get a pet yet.

Connie: Haha... Yeah, you're right. Let's get some food and talk about it.

25. Expresando Tu Opinion – Expressing Your Opinion

Jake: ¿Dónde deberíamos tomar vacaciones este año? Necesitamos decidir pronto.

Melissa: Bueno, me gustaría ir a un lugar cálido. ¿Qué tal la playa? O podríamos alquilar una cabaña en el lago.

Jake: ¿Quieres ir a la playa, otra vez? Quiero esquiar este invierno. ¿Podemos llegar a un acuerdo y viajar a las Rocky Mountains en Colorado el próximo mes de abril? Hay hermosos centros de esquí allí.

Melissa: ¡Oh, nunca hemos estado en Colorado antes! Pero no sé si será soleado y cálido para ese entonces. Primero necesito investigar un poco. Eso me ayudará a tomar una decisión.

EXPRESSING YOUR OPINION

Jake: Where should we take a vacation this year? We need to decide soon.

Melissa: Well, I'd like to go somewhere warm. How about the beach? Or we could rent a cabin on the lake.

Jake: You want to go to the beach, again? I want to ski this winter. We can compromise and travel to the Rocky Mountains in Colorado next April? There are beautiful ski resorts there.

Melissa: Oh, we've never been to Colorado before! But I don't know if it will be sunny and warm then. I need to do some research first. That will help me make a decision.

26. Pasatiempos – Hobbies

Ryan: Estoy tan feliz de que esta semana de exámenes haya terminado.

Tyler: Siento lo mismo. Tengo muchas ganas de relajarme en las montañas este fin de semana. He planeado una pequeña caminata en el bosque. Si el tiempo es bueno, me voy a ir haciendo canotaje por el río también.

Ryan: ¡Oh, que divertido! Voy a Colorado. Me llevo mi cámara porque el otoño viene rápido. Las hojas ya están transformando todos sus tonos en rojo y naranja. Será asombroso.

Tyler: La próxima vez que vayas allí, te acompañaré. Escuché que Colorado es un gran lugar para el piragüismo.

HOBBIES

Ryan: I'm so happy this week of midterm exams is finished.

Tyler: Same here. I'm looking forward to relaxing in the mountains this weekend. I've planned a nice little hike in the woods. Also, if the weather is good, I'm going to go canoeing down the river.

Ryan: Oh, how fun! I'm going to Colorado. I'm taking my camera because fall is coming fast. The leaves are already turning all shades of red and orange. It will be awesome.

Tyler: Next time you go there, I'll join you. I've heard Colorado is a great place to go canoeing.

27. La Boda – The Wedding

Angélica: ¿No se ve hermosa la novia en ese vestido de novia?

Maria: Sí. Ella se ve increíble. Y el novio es muy romántico.

¡Acabo de escuchar la historia de cómo se comprometieron! Le propuso matrimonio durante una cena a la luz de las velas en Praga. Ese fue el lugar en donde fueron a la escuela.

Angelica: ¿Oh sí? Maravilloso. ¡Y la luna de miel! ¡Que buena idea! La mayoría de las personas simplemente van a la playa por una semana después de casarse. Creo que es una idea tan aburrida. En cambio planean dirigirse a California y recorrer la costa en su motocicleta.

Maria: ¡De verdad! Qué idea tan fantástica. Ésta es sin duda la mejor boda en la que he estado en mi vida!

THE WEDDING

Angelica: Doesn't the bride look beautiful in that wedding dress?

Maria: Yes. She looks amazing. And the groom is such a romantic.

I just heard the story of how they got engaged! He proposed to her during a candlelight dinner in Prague. That was where they went to school.

Angelica: Oh yea? Wonderful. And the honeymoon! What a great idea! Most people just go to the beach for a week after they tie the knot. I think that's such a boring idea. Instead, they plan on going to California and cruising the coast on their motorcycle.

Maria: Really! What a fantastic idea. This is by far the best wedding I've ever been to in my life!

28. DAR CONSEJOS – GIVING ADVICE

Layla: Gracias por reunirte conmigo durante tu hora del almuerzo. Lo aprecio.

Monica: No hay problema. Estoy feliz de ayudar ¿Que está pasando?

Layla: Oh ya sabes, lo de siempre. Tengo que decidir pronto… ¿Debería tomar este nuevo trabajo? ¿O me quedo con mi trabajo actual?

Monica: Bueno, creo que es hora de un cambio, ¿verdad? Te pagan tarde y no estás feliz. Son razones suficientes para dejar tu trabajo.

Layla: ¿De verdad piensas eso?

Monica: Así, así es. Y hace más de un año que te escucho quejándote. Créeme. Toma el trabajo. ¿Qué tienes que perder?

Layla: Ok, me convenciste. Siempre me has dado los mejores consejos.

GIVING ADVICE

Layla: Thanks for meeting with me during your lunch hour. I appreciate it.

Monica: No problem. I'm happy to help. What's happening?

Layla: Oh you know, the usual. I have to decide soon... Should I take this new job? Or do I stick with my current one?

Monica: Well, I think it's time for a change, don't you? They pay you late and you are unhappy. That's more than enough reasons to quit your job.

Layla: Do you really think so?

Monica: I know so. And I've been listening to you complain for over a year now. Trust me. Take the job. What do you have to lose?

Layla: Ok, you convinced me. You have always given me the best advice.

29. Enseñando A Niños – Teaching Children

Sam: Hola Jack, ¿cómo estuvo tu día?

Jack: Hola Sam, ¿dónde has estado? Te estaba buscando.

Sam: No vas a creer la experiencia interesante que acabo de tener. ¡Pasé todo el día con una clase de estudiantes!

Jack: Eso suena divertido. Dime más.

Sam: Sí, fue un gran momento ... ¡pero fue tan agotador! No creí que los niños pudiesen tener tanta energía.

Jack: ¿Dónde conociste a todos estos niños?

Sam: en la escuela primaria en Chicago. Tuve la oportunidad de ir a algunas de sus clases por la mañana. Después de eso, les enseñé algo básico de inglés con juegos de palabras en la tarde.

Jack: Estoy seguro de que el inglés probablemente fue muy difícil para ellos.

Sam: Sorprendentemente, todos estaban ansiosos por aprender. Honestamente, estaba impresionado.

Jack: Eso es genial. ¿Qué terminaste enseñándoles?

Sam: ¡A los niños les encanta repetir cosas en voz alta! Algunas veces gritaba las oraciones y me gritaban. Susurré, y ellos me susurraron. ¡Fue muy divertido!

Jack: Cuando era estudiante de intercambio, nunca tuvimos clases de inglés así. Me alegra que los niños hayan tenido una experiencia tan maravillosa.

TEACHING CHILDREN

Sam: Hi Jack, how was your day?

Jack: Hi Sam, where have you been? I've been looking for you.

Sam: You won't believe the interesting experience I just had. I spent the whole day with a ton of children!

Jack: That sounds like fun. Tell me more.

Sam: Yes, it was a great time... but it was so exhausting! I didn't realize that kids have so much energy.

Jack: Where did you meet all these kids?

Sam: At the elementary school in Chicago. I had an opportunity to visit some of their classes in the morning. After that I taught them some basic English with word games in the afternoon.

Jack: I'm sure English was probably very difficult for them.

Sam: Surprisingly, they were all very eager to learn. Honestly, I was impressed.

Jack: That's great. What did you end up teaching them?

Sam: The kids love to repeat things out loud! Sometimes I yelled out the sentences, and they yelled back at me. I whispered, and they whispered back. It was so much fun!

Jack: You know, when I was a foreign exchange student, we never had English lessons like that. It makes me happy the children had such a wonderful experience.

30. Diversión Jugando Al Tenis – Fun With Tennis

Alma: Sebastian, ¿podrías mostrarme cómo sostener el raqueta?

Sebastian: Claro Alma, es como cuando nos damos la mano. Extiende la mano como si estuvieras a punto de estrechar mi mano...

Alma: ¿Solo así?

Sebastian: Sí, solo así. Ahora, pon la raqueta en la mano, así.

Alma: ¡Ahora estoy lista para pegarle a la pelota como un profesional!

Sebastian: Jaja, ¡casi! Recuerda lo que te dije. Solo hay dos tipos de cambios, el golpe de derecha y el revés.

Alma: Ok, recuerdo. Dijiste que golpear con la derecha, comenzando desde la derecha, es como golpear una pelota de ping pong.

Sebastian: Eso es correcto. Pruébalo ahora. ¿Estás lista? ¡Golpea esto!

Alma: ¡Ufa! ¡Lo falle completamente!

Sebastian: Está bien, intenta de nuevo.

Alma: Oh, ya veo. Déjame intentar de nuevo...

Sebastian: Aquí viene otra pelota... ¡Guau! ¡La golpeas sobre la valla! Eres una mujer muy poderosa.

Alma: Jaja. ¡Creo que necesito practicar más!

FUN WITH TENNIS

Alma: Sebastian, could you show me how to hold the racket?

Sebastian: Sure Alma, it's just like when we shake hands. Hold your hand out as if you were about to shake my hand...

Alma: Just like this?

Sebastian: Yes, just like that. Now, put the racket in your hand, like this.

Alma: Now I'm ready to hit the ball like a professional!

Sebastian: Haha, almost! Remember what I told you. There are only two types of swings, the forehand and the backhand.

Alma: Ok, I remember. You said hitting a forehand, starting on my right, is like hitting a ping pong ball.

Sebastian: That's right. Give it a try now. Are you ready? Hit this!

Alma: Oops! I completely missed it!

Sebastian: That's alright, try again.

Alma: Oh, I see. Let me try again...

Sebastian: Here comes another ball... Wow! You hit it over the fence! You're a very powerful lady.

Alma: Haha. I guess I need to practice more!

31. Viviendo En California – Living In California

Jessica: Hace tanto frío esta mañana.

Tatiana: Así es. Temprano esta mañana tuve que rociar el parabrisas de mi auto porque estaba cubierto de escarcha.

Jessica: Nunca pensé que podría ser tan frío a principios de diciembre, especialmente en California.

Tatiana: Lo sé. La temperatura era de 40 grados Fahrenheit cuando me desperté esta mañana. Me estaba helando tan pronto como me levanté de la cama. El clima frío definitivamente no fue una agradable sorpresa.

Jessica: No recuerdo cuándo fue tan frío en diciembre.

Tatiana: Lo que es peor es que va a llover esta tarde. ¡Va a ser frío y húmedo!

Jessica: ¡Puaj!¿Va a llover esta tarde?

Tatiana: No solo esta tarde, sino también el resto de la semana. La noticia decía que comenzaría a lloviznar justo antes del mediodía, y que va a llover muy fuerte a las cuatro en punto.

Jessica: ¿Supongo que no hay señales de mejor clima esta semana?

Tatiana: Existe una pequeña posibilidad de que llegue el sol para el sábado. Sin embargo, habrá neblina, viento y lluvia antes de que salga el sol este fin de semana.

Jessica: Me alegro de que llueva aunque no me gusta el clima lluvioso. Hemos tenido una temporada muy seca lo que va de este año.

Tatiana: Sí, apenas recuerdo cuándo llovió la última vez. Bueno, mientras no haya truenos ni relámpagos, puedo soportarlo.

Jessica: Rara vez tenemos truenos o rayos en California.

Tatiana: Tenemos mucha suerte de que California tenga una de las mejores condiciones climáticas de América.

Jessica: Tienes razón, hay peores lugares en los que podríamos estar viviendo. Bien, la clase está comenzando ahora, así que nos vemos más tarde.

Tatiana: Hasta luego.

LIVING IN CALIFORNIA

Jessica: It is so chilly this morning.

Tatiana: It certainly is. Early this morning I had to spray my car's windshield because it was covered with frost.

Jessica: I never would have thought it could be this cold in early December, especially in California.

Tatiana: I know. The temperature was 40 degrees Fahrenheit when I woke up this morning. I was freezing as soon as I got out of bed. The cold weather was definitely not a nice surprise.

Jessica: I can't remember when it was actually this cold in December.

Tatiana: What's worse is that it's going to rain this afternoon. It's going to be cold and wet!

Jessica: Yuck! It's going to rain this afternoon?

Tatiana: Not just this afternoon, but also the entire rest of the week. The news said that it would start to drizzle just before noon, and then it would rain really hard by four o'clock.

Jessica: I'm guessing there's no sign of better weather this week?

Tatiana: There is a slim chance of sunshine by Saturday. However, it will be foggy, windy, and rainy before the sun comes out this weekend.

Jessica: I am glad that it rains even though I do not like rainy weather. We have a very dry season so far this year.

Tatiana: Yes, I can hardly remember when it rained last time. Well, as long as there is no thunder or lightning, I can stand it.

Jessica: We rarely have thunder or lightning in California.

Tatiana: We are very lucky that California has one of the best weather conditions in America.

Jessica: You are right, there are worse places we could be living. Alright, class is starting right now so I'll see you later.

Tatiana: See you later.

32. HORNEANDO – BAKING GOODNESS

Chelsea: Mamá, ¿qué estás cocinando? Huele tan bien.

Sra. Kelly: Estoy horneando pasteles. Esta es tu tarta de zanahoria favorita.

Chelsea: Se ve deliciosa. Y veo magdalenas por allí también. Has estado ocupada, ¿verdad?

Sra. Kelly: Sí. Donovan tiene que llevar algunas a una fiesta de cumpleaños mañana. Entonces, esas magdalenas son solo para él. No te las comas.

Chelsea: ¿Puedo tomar un pedazo de pastel de zanahoria? Quiero disfrutar la vida ahora mismo.

Sra. Kelly: ¿No quieres esperar hasta después de cenar?

Chelsea: El pastel está llamando mi nombre, "Chelsea, cómeme ... cómeme ..." No, no quiero esperar. ¿Puedo, mamá?

Sra. Kelly: Ja, ja ... Ok, adelante.

Chelsea: ¡Mmm! Entonces, ¿qué hay para cenar esta noche?

Sra. Kelly: Preparé carne asada y crema de champiñones.

Chelsea: Ha pasado mucho tiempo desde que preparaste sopa de champiñones. ¿Necesitas ayuda, mamá?

Sra. Kelly: No, ve a hacer tu tarea y déjame cocinar.

Chelsea: Gracias, mamá. Llámame cuando la cena esté lista. No quiero llegar tarde a la carne asada, sopa de champiñones, pastel de zanahoria y magdalenas.

Sra. Kelly: Las magdalenas son para Donovan. ¡No las toques!

Chelsea: Lo sé, mamá. Es una broma.

BAKING GOODNESS

Chelsea: Mom, what are you cooking? It smells so good.

Mrs. Kelly: I am baking cakes. This is your favorite carrot cake.

Chelsea: It looks scrumptious. And I see muffins some over there too. You have been busy, haven't you?

Mrs. Kelly: Yes. Donovan has to take some to a birthday party tomorrow. So, those muffins are just for him. Don't eat them.

Chelsea: Can I have a piece of carrot cake? I want to enjoy life right now.

Mrs. Kelly: You don't want to wait until after dinner?

Chelsea: The cake is calling my name, "Chelsea, eat me... eat me..." No, I don't want to wait. Can I, mom?

Mrs. Kelly: Ha ha... Ok, go ahead.

Chelsea: Yum! So what's for dinner tonight?

Mrs. Kelly: I will make roast beef and cream of mushroom soup.

Chelsea: It has been a long time since you made cream of mushroom soup. Do you need any help, mom?

Mrs. Kelly: No, go do your homework and leave the cooking to me.

Chelsea: Thanks, mom. Call me whenever dinner is ready. I do not want to be late for roast beef, cream of mushroom soup, carrot cake and muffins.

Mrs. Kelly: The muffins are for Donovan. Do not touch them!

Chelsea: I know, mom. I'm just kidding.

33. Ayuda Por Teléfono – Help Over The Phone

Gigi: Gracias por llamar al Sports Recreation Center. ¿Como puedo ayudarte?

Colette: Compré una bicicleta de ejercicio en su tienda hace un par de meses y estoy teniendo problemas con ella. Dejó de funcionar y necesito que la reparen.

Gigi: Déjame conectarte con el departamento de Servicio. Un momento por favor.

Angela: Departamento de servicio, soy Angela. ¿Como puedo ayudarle?

Colette: Compré una bicicleta de ejercicio en el Sports Center el año pasado y debe ser reparada.

Angela: ¿Cuál parece ser el problema?

Colette: No sé lo que sucedió, pero la pantalla de la computadora está en negro y ya no se enciende.

Angela: ¿Intentó presionar el botón de comenzar?

Colette: Sí, y nada se enciende.

Angela: ¿Cuál es el modelo de la bicicleta?

Colette: Es una Skull Crusher 420Z+, es la que tiene la cesta en la parte delantera.

Angela: Puedo enviar un técnico para echarle un vistazo a tu bicicleta. Costará $ 5000.00 por mano de obra. Además, si tenemos que reemplazar alguna pieza, eso será adicional. ¿Suena como un trato?

Colette: Eso es caro. ¿El costo de reparación no está cubierto por la garantía?

Angela: ¿Cuándo compraste tu bicicleta?

Colette: Hace aproximadamente tres meses.

Angela: Lo siento. La garantía estándar solo cubre por un mes. ¿Usted compró una cobertura de garantía adicional en el momento de la compra?

Colette: No, no lo hice. ¿Hay otras opciones en vez de pagar $5,000.00 por el trabajo de reparación?

Angela: No, me temo que no.

Colette: ¡Demonios!

HELP OVER THE PHONE

Gigi: Thank you for calling Sports Recreation Center. How may I help you?

Colette: I purchased an exercise bike from your store a couple months ago, and I am having problems with it. It stopped working and I need to have it repaired.

Gigi: Let me connect you to the Service department. One moment please.

Angela: Service department, this is Angela. How can I help you?

Colette: I bought an exercise bike from Sports Center last year and it needs to be repaired.

Angela: What seems to be the problem?

Colette: I am not what happened, but the computer screen is black and doesn't turn on anymore.

Angela: Did you try to press the Start button?

Colette: Yes, and nothing turns on.

Angela: What is your bike model?

Colette: It is a Skull Crusher 420Z+, it's the one with the really cool basket in the front.

Angela: I can send a technician out to take a look at your bike. It will cost $5,000.00 for labor. Also, if we have to replace any parts, that will be extra. Sound like a deal?

Colette: That is expensive. Isn't the repair cost covered by warranty?

Angela: When did you purchase your bike?

Colette: About 3 months ago.

Angela: I am sorry. The standard warranty only covers 1 month. Did you buy extra warranty coverage at the time of purchase?

Colette: No, I did not. Are there any other options besides paying $5,000.00 for repair labor?

Angela: No, I am afraid not.

Colette: Damnit.

34. Vamos A Un Concierto – Let's Go To A Concert

Keith: Hola Danielle, Simon, hay un concierto en el parque esta noche con una gran banda. ¿Quieren ir?

Danielle: No trabajo esta noche, así que definitivamente puedo ir.

Simon: ¡Yo también, vamos!

Danielle: Hay muchos autos en la calle esta noche ...

Simon: Sí, ¿por qué el tráfico es tan intenso?

Keith: La gente probablemente se dirige hacia el parque para el concierto. Es una banda muy popular y tocan muy buena música.

Danielle: Sí, lo hacen. Durante los últimos cuatro años, nunca me he perdido ninguno de sus conciertos. Cada vez que descubro que la banda viene a la ciudad, compro un boleto de inmediato.

Simon: ¿Hace cuánto que la banda comenzó a tocar aquí localmente?

Danielle: Comenzaron una tradición hace seis años y ahora todos los años tocan toda la primera semana de junio.

Keith: Simon, vas a disfrutar esta noche. Habrá buena música, muchos saltos y definitivamente muchos gritos. Incluso pueden tener un pogo.

Simon: No aguanto más, suena muy divertido

Danielle: Mi favorita es la música "gangster rap"; sin embargo, debo decir que la música country puede ser agradable de escuchar. Sorprendentemente, puedo escucharlo todo el día.

Keith: Simon, ¿qué tipo de música te gusta?

Simon: Oh, me gusta todo tipo de música siempre que no sea agresivo.

Danielle: ¡Guau, el estadio está lleno de gente! Estoy sorprendido de la cantidad de personas que ya se presentaron al concierto. ¡Es bueno que ya estemos aquí!

LET'S GO TO A CONCERT

Keith: Hey Danielle, Simon, there is a concert in the park tonight with a great line up. Do you want to go?

Danielle: I don't work tonight so I can definitely go.

Simon: Me too, let's go!

Danielle: There's a ton of cars out tonight...

Simon: Yea, why is the traffic so heavy?

Keith: People are probably heading toward the park for the concert. It's a very popular band and they play really good music.

Danielle: Yes, they do. For the last four years, I have never missed one of their concerts. Every time I find out that the band is coming to town I buy a ticket right away.

Simon: How long ago did the band start playing here locally?

Danielle: They started a tradition six years ago and now every year they play the whole first week of June.

Keith: Simon, you are really going to enjoy this evening. There will be good great music, a lot of jumping around, and definitely a lot of shouting. They may even have a mosh pit.

Simon: I can't wait, it sounds like a lot fun.

Danielle: My favorite is gangster rap music; however, I have to say that country music can be pleasant to listen to. Surprisingly, I can listen to it all day long.

Keith: Simon, what kind of music do you like?

Simon: Oh, I like all kinds of music as long as it is not aggressive.

Danielle: Wow, the stadium is packed with people! I'm surprised at the number of people who have already shown up for the concert. It's a good thing we're here already!

35. Haciendo Planes – Making Plans

Connie: Lisa, dime... ¿Cuáles son tus planes para este próximo fin de semana?

Lisa: No lo sé. ¿Quieres unirte y hacer algo?

Sarah: ¿Qué te parece ir a ver una película? AMC 24 en Parker Road está presentando *Si Me Dejas, Te Borro*.

Connie: ¡He estado esperando mucho para verla! Es como si leyeras mi mente. ¿Quieres salir a cenar antes?

Sarah: Me parece perfecto. ¿Dónde quieres que nos encontremos?

Lisa: Nos vemos en la Red Rooster House. Ha pasado un tiempo desde que estuve allí.

Connie: Buena idea otra vez. Escuché que tienen una nueva pasta. Debería ser bueno porque Red Rooster House siempre tiene la mejor comida italiana de la ciudad.

Sarah: ¿Cuándo deberíamos encontrarnos?

Lisa: Bueno, la película está a las 2:00 p.m., a las 4:00 p.m., a las 6:00 p.m. y a las 8:00 p.m.

Connie: ¿Por qué no vamos al show de las 4:00 p.m.? Podemos encontrarnos en Red Rooster House a la 1 p.m. Eso nos dará suficiente tiempo.

MAKING PLANS

Connie: Lisa, tell me... What are your plans for this upcoming weekend?

Lisa: I don't know. Do you want to get together and do something?

Sarah: How do you feel about going to see a movie? AMC 24 on Parker Road is showing *If You Leave Me, I Delete You*.

Connie: I've been wanting to see that! It's like you read my mind. Do you want to go out to dinner beforehand?

Sarah: That's fine with me. Where do you want to meet?

Lisa: Let's meet at the Red Rooster House. It's been a while since I've been there.

Connie: Good idea again. I heard they just came out with a new pasta. It should be good because Red Rooster House always has the best Italian food in town.

Sarah: When should we meet?

Lisa: Well, the movie is showing at 1:00PM, 2:00PM, 4:00PM and 6:00PM.

Connie: Why don't we go to the 4:00PM show? We can meet at Red Rooster House at 1PM. That will give us enough time.

36. Receso invernal – Winter Break

Trent: Hola Jared, si estás listo para ir, pon todas tus cosas en el baúl y montate en el asiento delantero.

Jared: Bien, Trent. Gracias por llevarme a casa. Usualmente mis padres me recogen, pero tenían que trabajar hasta tarde esta noche.

Trent: No hay problema, me alegro de poder ayudarte.

Jared: Por cierto, ¿Cuándo es nuestro próximo juego de baloncesto?

Trent: Es después de las vacaciones de invierno, pero aún falta mucho para eso. ¿Has hecho algún plan para las vacaciones?

Jared: No, no todavía. Además de ir a la práctica de baloncesto, voy a estar trabajando.

Trent: ¿Trabajando? ¿Conseguiste un nuevo trabajo o sigues trabajando en Twisters?

Jared: Bueno, Twisters fue un buen primer trabajo y la gente fue realmente genial. Sin embargo, el horario era muy exigente y para mí era difícil ir a la escuela y al trabajo.

Trent: Bueno, ¿qué estás haciendo ahora en tu nuevo trabajo?

Jared: Estoy trabajando en ventas de tecnología. Está en un centro de atención telefónica. Al principio fue un poco difícil, pero ahora estoy acostumbrado a hablar con desconocidos por teléfono.

Trent: Oh, eso suena genial. ¿Cuándo comenzaste el nuevo trabajo?

Jared: He estado con Techmerica desde el 1 de octubre. ¿Tienes algún plan para las vacaciones?

Trent: Estoy planeando un viaje de snowboarding a Aspen. Deberías venir si no estás demasiado ocupado en el nuevo trabajo.

Jared: ¡Oh, eso suena divertido! Gracias por la invitación.

WINTER BREAK

Trent: Hey Jared, if you're ready to go just throw your all of your stuff in the trunk and ride in the front seat.

Jared: Alright, Trent. Thank you for giving me a ride home. Usually my parents pick me up, but they had to work late tonight.

Trent: No worries, I'm glad I could help.

Jared: By the way, when is our next basketball game?

Trent: It is sometime after winter break, but anyways it's a long time from now. Have you made any plans for the break though?

Jared: Not really. Other than going to basketball practice, I'll just be working.

Trent: Working? Did you get a new job or are you still working at Twisters?

Jared: Well, Twisters was a good first job and the people were really great to work with. However, the schedule was very demanding which made it difficult to go to school and work.

Trent: Well, what are you doing now at your new job?

Jared: I am working in technology sales. It's at a call center. It was a little difficult at first, but now I am used to talking to strangers on the phone.

Trent: Oh, that sounds great. When did you start the new job?

Jared: I have been with Techmerica since October 1st. Do you have any plans for break?

Trent: I am planning a snowboarding trip to Aspen. You should come if you're not too busy at the new job.

Jared: Oh, that sounds like fun! Thank you for the invitation.

37. Visitar Al Doctor – Visiting The Doctor

Doctor: Buenos días, Amy.

Amy: Buenos días, doctor.

Doctor: Al ver su información, veo que usted comenzó a sentirse cansada hace un mes, y luego comenzó a tener migraña.

¿Ha tenido fiebre y malestar estomacal también?

Amy: No, doctor.

Doctor: Déjeme hacer un chequeo físico rápido.

Doctor: Por favor, respire profundo, contenga la respiración y luego exhale. Una vez más por favor.

Doctor: ¿Ha realizado algún cambio en su dieta al observar la fluctuación en su peso recientemente?

Amy: He perdido cinco libras recientemente, pero no he cambiado mi dieta en absoluto.

Doctor: ¿Por casualidad usted sufre de insomnio?

Amy: Es difícil quedarme dormida cuando me voy a la cama. También me despierto mucho durante la noche.

Doctor: ¿Bebe o fuma cigarrillos?

Amy: No.

Doctor: Parece que usted tiene neumonía. Además de eso, no veo ningún otro problema. Por ahora, descansa un poco y haz algo de ejercicio. Voy a darle una receta para la neumonía. ¿Es usted alérgica a algún medicamento?

Amy: No que yo sepa.

Doctor: Bien. Tome este medicamento tres veces al día después de comer.

Amy: Gracias, doctor.

Doctor: De nada.

Visiting The Doctor

Doctor: Good morning, Amy.

Amy: Good morning, Doctor.

Doctor: Looking at your information, I see that you started feeling tired about a month ago, and then you started having migraines.

You have also had an upset stomach and fever?

Amy: No, doctor.

Doctor: Let me do a quick physical checkup.

Doctor: Please take a deep breath, hold your breath, and then exhale. One more time please.

Doctor: Have you made any changes to your diet seen fluctuation in your weight recently?

Amy: I lost five pounds recently, but I haven't changed my diet at all.

Doctor: By chance do you suffer from insomnia?

Amy: It is difficult for me to fall asleep when I go to bed. I also wake up a lot during the night.

Doctor: Do you drink or smoke cigarettes?

Amy: No.

Doctor: It appears that you have pneumonia. Besides that, I do not see any other problems. For now, get some rest and do some exercise.

I am going to give you a prescription for the pneumonia. Are you allergic to any medications?

Amy: Not that I am aware of.

Doctor: Alright. Take this medication three times a day after you eat.

Amy: Thank you, Doctor.

Doctor: You are welcome.

38. El Mercado – The Market

Laura: Joy, antes de que mamá se fue al trabajo esta mañana, me pidió que comprara unas cosas en el supermercado. El problema es que necesito terminar mi proyecto escolar. ¿Puedes ir por mí?

Joy: He terminado con mis tareas, así que puedo ir al supermercado por ti. ¿Qué quería mamá que compraras?

Laura: Además de pollo, pescado y verduras, podemos comprar cualquier cosa que queramos para los refrigerios y para el desayuno. Ella básicamente quería que comprara suficientes alimentos para toda la semana.

Joy: ¿Hay algo que quieras específicamente para desayunar?

Laura: Supongo que algo de harina de avena, como de costumbre.

Joy: No quiero avena todos los días. Voy a comprar algunos panqueques y jarabe, entonces.

Laura: Si puedes encontrarlo, obtén los nuevos panqueques sin gluten en la sección de salud, por favor. Quiero ver si saben diferente.

Joy: ¿Todavía hay suficiente café y crema para mamá y papá?

Laura: Sí, hay bastante. De hecho, también debes comprar leche. Casi se nos acaba de eso.

Joy: Además de eso, ¿qué quieres como bocadillos?

Laura: Algunas papas fritas estarían bien. Probablemente quieras tus galletas de chocolate.

Joy: Es mejor que yo escriba todas estas cosas o las olvidaré cuando llegue al mercado. ¡Odiaría tener que hacer dos viajes!

THE MARKET

Laura: Joy, before mom left for work this morning she asked me to go grocery shopping. The problem is that I need to finish my school project. Can you go for me?

Joy: I am finished with my chores, so I can go to the store for you. What did mom want you to buy?

Laura: Besides chicken, fish and vegetables, we can buy whatever else we want for snacks and breakfast. She basically wanted me to buy enough groceries for the entire week.

Joy: Is there anything specifically you want for breakfast?

Laura: I guess some oatmeal as usual.

Joy: I don't want oatmeal every day. I will buy some pancakes and syrup then.

Laura: If you can find it, get the new gluten free pancakes in the health section please. I want to see if it tastes any different.

Joy: Is there still enough coffee and cream for mom and dad?

Laura: Yes, we do. In fact, you should buy some milk also. We almost out of it.

Joy: Next, what do you want for snacks?

Laura: Some chips would be fine with me. You probably want your chocolate cookies.

Joy: Knowing myself it's probably better that I write all these things down or else I will forget them by the time I get to the market. I would hate to have to make two trips!

39. Obtengamos Un Apartamento – Let's Get An Apartment

Patrick: Hola, Josh. ¿Qué estás haciendo aquí?

Josh: Estoy buscando un apartamento para alquilar. ¿Qué estás haciendo aquí? ¿Estás buscando un apartamento también?

Patrick: Sí. La casa de mis padres está muy lejos, así que me gustaría encontrar un apartamento que esté más cerca de la escuela y de mi trabajo.

Josh: Ok, eso tiene sentido. Todavía no he decidido si quiero quedarme en los dormitorios o conseguir mi propio apartamento.

Patrick: Entonces, ¿qué estás buscando?

Josh: No necesito mucho para ser honesto. Todo lo que necesito es un lugar lo suficientemente grande para mi cama y mi escritorio. Por supuesto, el lugar necesita una cocina para poder cocinar. Así puedo ahorrar un algo de dinero.

Patrick: Eso suena como lo que estoy buscando también. No puedo trabajar a tiempo completo como lo hice durante el verano. Pasaré la mayor parte del tiempo estudiando, así no podré trabajar tanto. Todo lo que necesito es algo seguro, tranquilo y limpio.

Josh: El otro problema para mí es pagar un apartamento completo. La mayoría de los lugares que he visto son muy caros.

Patrick: ¿Has pensado en compartir un apartamento? Si lo deseas, podemos encontrar un apartamento de dos habitaciones y compartirlo. Puede ser más barato de esa manera.

Josh: Eso podría resolver nuestro problema. ¿Quieres probarlo?

Patrick: Sí, podría ser una gran idea. Vamos a ver este apartamento y así decidir si nos gusta.

Let's Get An Apartment

Patrick: Hey, Josh. What are you doing here?

Josh: I am looking for an apartment to rent. What are you doing here? Are you looking for an apartment also?

Patrick: Yes. My parents' house is really far away so I'd like to find an apartment that is closer to school and my job.

Josh: Ok, that makes sense. I still haven't decided if I want to stay in the dorms or get my own apartment.

Patrick: So, what are you looking for?

Josh: I don't need much to be honest. All I need is a place big enough for my bed and desk. Of course, it needs to have a kitchen so that I can cook my meals and save a little bit of money.

Patrick: That sounds like what I'm looking for too. I can't work full-time like I did during the summer. I will be spending most of my time studying so I won't be able to work as much. All I need is something safe, quiet and clean.

Josh: The other issue is paying for an entire apartment for myself. Most places I have seen are very expensive.

Patrick: Have you thought about sharing an apartment? If you want, we can find a two-bedroom apartment and share it. It may be cheaper that way.

Josh: That could solve our problem. Do you want to try it?

Patrick: Yes, that could be a great idea. Let's go check this one out and see if we like it.

40. El Quiosco – The Concesssion Stand

Simon: Hay un puesto de comida allí. ¿Quieren algo?

Danielle: Nada para mí, gracias. Ya tengo mi botella de agua.

Keith: Quiero una bolsa de papas fritas y una cerveza fría. ¿Estás segura de que no quieres un perro caliente, Danielle?

Danielle: Estoy bastante segura. Mi madre está cocinando una buena cena de bistec y quiero asegurarme de no comer demasiado aquí.

Keith: Danielle, eres muy afortunada de tener una buena cocinera como madre. Simon, tienes que probar su pastel de arándanos uno de estos días. Honestamente, no hay mejor pastel en toda esta ciudad.

Danielle: ¡De hecho, mi madre está cocinando su pastel de arándanos esta noche! Me gustaría, te guardaré una pieza, Simon.

Simon: ¡Espero que no estés bromeando con semejante regalo! Me encantaría un pedazo.

Danielle: ¿Qué hay de ti, Keith? ¿Un pedazo de pastel para ti también?

Simon: Keith, será mejor que consigas tus bocadillos y cerveza ahora si aún los quieres. Son casi las 3:00 p.m, y el espectáculo está a punto de comenzar.

Keith: Última oportunidad de conseguir algo. ¿Están seguros de que no quieren nada?

Danielle: Estoy segura, gracias Keith.

Simon: Yo también estoy seguro, Keith.

Keith: Ok, guarda mi asiento y ya vuelvo pronto.

THE CONCESSION STAND

Simon: There is a food stand over there. Do you two want anything?

Danielle: Nothing for me, thanks. I already have my bottle of water.

Keith: I want a bag of chips and a cold beer. Are you sure you do not want a hot dog, Danielle?

Danielle: I am quite sure. My mom is cooking a good steak dinner, and I want to make sure I don't eat too much here.

Keith: Danielle, you are so lucky to have such a good cook for a mother. Simon, you have to taste her blueberry pie one of these days. Honestly, there's no better pie in this whole town.

Danielle: In fact, my mom is baking her blueberry pie tonight! I you would like, I will save you a piece, Simon.

Simon: Don't tease me with a good time! I would love that.

Danielle: How about you, Keith? A piece of cake for you too?

Simon: Keith, you better get your snacks and beer now if you still want them. It is almost 3:00PM, and the show is about to start.

Keith: Last chance to get something. Are you guys sure you don't want anything?

Danielle: I am sure, thank you Keith.

Simon: Me neither, Keith.

Keith: Ok, save my seat and I will be right back.

41. El Almuerzo – Lunchtime

Emily: Tricia, ¿me prestas tu móvil para llamar a mi madre después del almuerzo?

Tricia: Sí, por supuesto, Emily. No te olvides de decirle mandarle un saludo de nuestra parte.

Maira: Emily, ¿podrías pasar la pimienta, por favor?

Emily: Seguro, aquí tienes.

Maira: Y la sal también, por favor. Gracias.

Emily: De nada.

Tricia: ¿Te importaría si pasamos por la librería Strand mientras vamos camino a la película?

Emily: No, en lo absoluto.

Maira: Escuché que tiene una nueva selección de libros, así que me encantaría pasar y comprobarlo.

Tricia: Pedí demasiada comida. ¿Alguien le gustaría probar algo de mi comida?

Emily: Sí, me gustaría un poco. Se ve deliciosa.

Tricia: ¿Y tú, Maira?

Maira: No, gracias. Ya tengo suficiente comida.

Emily: Tricia, ¿te gustaría probar una de mis fajitas?

Tricia: Sí, por favor.

Emily: Aquí tienes. ¿Quieres otra?

Tricia: ¡Oh, eso es más que suficiente! Gracias.

Maira: ¿Me imagino que todos hemos terminado de comer? Deberíamos irnos ahora para evitar el tráfico, sino llegaremos tarde.

Tricia: Estoy lista para irme cuando ustedes estén listas.

Emily: Yo también. Vámonos.

LUNCHTIME

Emily: Tricia, May I borrow your cell phone to call my mother after lunch?

Tricia: Yes, of course, Emily. Don't forget to tell her we said hello.

Maira: Emily, could you pass the pepper, please?

Emily: Certainly, here you are.

Maira: And the salt too, please. Thank you.

Emily: You're welcome.

Tricia: Would either of you mind if we stop by Strand Bookstore on the way to the movie?

Emily: No, not at all.

Maira: I heard they have a new book selection so I would love to stop by and check it out.

Tricia: I ordered too much food. Would anybody care to try some of my food?

Emily: Yes, I would like some. It looks delicious.

Tricia: How about you, Maira?

Maira: No, thank you. I have enough food already.

Emily: Tricia, would you like to taste one of my fajitas?

Tricia: Yes, please.

Emily: Here you go. Do you want another?

Tricia: Oh, that is more than enough! Thank you.

Maira: I imagine we are all finished eating? We should leave now to avoid the traffic; otherwise we will be late.

Tricia: I am ready to leave whenever you all are.

Emily: So am I. Let's go.

42. Buscando Trabajo – Searching For A Job

Matilda: Hola John, es bueno verte.

John: Lo mismo digo, Matilda. Ha pasado mucho tiempo desde la última vez que te vi.

Matilda: Sí, la última vez que nos vimos fue en Halloween. ¿Cómo está todo?

John: Estoy bien. Sería mejor si tuviera un nuevo trabajo.

Matilda: ¿Por qué estás buscando un nuevo trabajo?

John: Bueno, me gradué la semana pasada. Ahora, quiero conseguir un trabajo en el campo de finanzas.

Matilda: ¿Has estado buscando un nuevo trabajo desde hace mucho?

John: Acabo de comenzar esta semana.

Matilda: Has preparado un curriculum vitae, ¿verdad?

John: Sí.

Matilda: Entonces, no te preocupes. Tienes mucha ambición y sé que pondrás toda tu energía en conseguir lo que quieras. Además, el mercado de trabajo es bueno en este momento, y todas las empresas necesitan analistas financieros.

John: Espero que sí. Gracias por el consejo.

SEARCHING FOR A JOB

Matilda: Hi Paolo, it is good to see you.

Paolo: Same here, Matilda. It has been a long time since I last saw you.

Matilda: Yes, the last time we saw each other was around Halloween. How is everything?

Paolo: I am doing OK. It would be better if I had a new job.

Matilda: Why are looking for a new job?

Paolo: Well, I graduated last week. Now, I want to get a job in the Finance field.

Matilda: Have you been looking for a new job for a while?

Paolo: I just started this week.

Matilda: You have prepared a resume, right?

Paolo: Yes.

Matilda: I wouldn't worry then. You have a lot of ambition and I know you will put all of your energy into getting what you want. Besides, the job market is really good right now, and all companies need financial analysts.

Paolo: I hope so. Thank you for the advice.

43. ENTREVISTA DE TRABAJO – JOB INTERVIEW

Hugh: Bienvenido Zach. Comencemos la entrevista. ¿Estás listo?

Zach: Sí, estoy listo.

Hugh: Genial. Antes que nada, permíteme presentarme adecuadamente. Soy el Gerente de Logística de la compañía. Necesito llenar un puesto de nivel de entrada lo antes posible.

Zach: Maravilloso. ¿Podría decirme un poco sobre la posición y sus expectativas?

Hugh: El nuevo empleado tendrá que trabajar exclusivamente con el departamento de fabricación. También existe el requisito de hablar con el banco diariamente.

Zach: ¿Cuáles son los requerimientos que necesita?

Hugh: Requiero un título universitario de cuatro años en administración de empresas. Alguna experiencia laboral previa sería útil.

Zach: ¿Qué tipo de experiencia usted está buscando?

Hugh: El trabajo general de la oficina está bien. La persona elegida no necesita mucha experiencia. Habrá entrenamiento en el trabajo para la persona adecuada.

Zach: ¡Eso es genial!

Hugh: ¿Cuáles son tus puntos fuertes? ¿Por qué debo contratarte?

Zach: Soy una persona trabajadora y aprendo rápido. Siempre estoy con ganas de aprender y me llevo bien con todos.

Hugh: Bien. No te importa trabajar muchas horas, ¿verdad?

Zach: No, no me importa en absoluto.

Hugh: ¿Puedes manejar el estrés?

Zach: Sí. Cuando iba a la escuela, tomaba 5 cursos cada semestre mientras trabajaba al menos veinticinco horas cada semana.

Hugh: ¿Tienes alguna pregunta para mí en este momento?

Zach: No, creo que entiendo muy bien el trabajo.

Hugh: Ok, Zach fue un placer conocerte. Gracias por venir.

Zach: Encantado de conocerlo también. Gracias por recibirme.

JOB INTERVIEW

Hugh: Welcome Zach. Let's start the interview. Are you ready?

Zach: Yes, I am.

Hugh: Great. First of all, let me properly introduce myself. I am the company Logistics Manager. I need to fill an entry-level position as soon as possible.

Zach: Wonderful. Could you tell me a little bit about the position and your expectations?

Hugh: The new employee will have to work closely with the manufacturing department. There is also a requirement to deal with the bank on a daily basis.

Zach: What type of qualifications do you require?

Hugh: I require a four-year college degree in business administration. Some previous work experience would be helpful.

Zach: What kind of experience are you looking for?

Hugh: General office work is fine. I do not require a lot of experience. There will be on the job training for the right person.

Zach: That is great!

Hugh: What are your strengths? Why should I hire you?

Zach: I am a hard-working person and a fast learner. I am very eager to learn, and I get along fine with everyone.

Hugh: Alright. You do not mind working long hours, do you?

Zach: No, I do not mind at all.

Hugh: Can you handle pressure?

Zach: Yes. When I was going to school, I took 5 courses each semester while working at least twenty-five hours every week.

Hugh: Do you have any questions for me at this time?

Zach: No, I think I have a pretty good understanding of the job.

Hugh: Ok, Zach it was nice meeting you. Thank you for coming.

Zach: Nice meeting you too. Thank you for seeing me.

44. Dando Una Presentación – Giving A Presentation

Sally: Tendré que dar una presentación sobre el calentamiento global el viernes, y estoy muy nerviosa.

Olga: Hay muchas cosas que puedes hacer para sentirte más segura y menos nerviosa.

Sally: ¿Qué debería hacer, Olga?

Olga: ¿Has investigado sobre el tema?

Sally: De hecho, he investigado mucho sobre el tema, y sé que puedo responder a casi todas las preguntas que recibiré de la audiencia.

Olga: Asegúrate de crear un esquema de tu presentación.

Sally: Tienes razón. Esto me ayudará a organizar toda la información.

Olga: Sí. Te ayudará a descubrir qué debería presentar primero, segundo, tercero...

Olga: ¡Buena idea! Es importante contar con hechos para respaldar tu presentación. Deseas que la presentación sea creíble.

Sally: ¡Voy a hacer eso ahora mismo! Gracias.

Olga: Tendrás una gran presentación.

Giving A Presentation

Sally: I will have to give a presentation on global warming on Friday, and I am so nervous.

Olga: There are a lot of things you can do to make you feel more confident and less nervous.

Sally: What should I do, Olga?

Olga: Have you done your research on the topic?

Sally: In fact, I have done a lot of research on the subject, and I know I can answer almost any questions I will receive from the audience.

Olga: Make sure to create an outline of your presentation.

Sally: You're right. This will help me organize all of the information.

Olga: Yes. It will help you figure out what should present first, second, third...

Olga: Good idea! It is important to have facts to support your presentation. You want the presentation to be credible.

Sally: I'm going to do that right now! Thank you.

Olga: You're going to have a great presentation.

45. Graduación – Graduation

Liz: Ese es un maravilloso ramo de flores. ¿Para quién es?

Annie: Estas flores son para mi hermana Silvia. Ella se gradúa hoy.

Liz: Debe haberte costado una fortuna.

Annie: Pagué setenta dólares por ellos.

Liz: Eso es bastante caro.

Annie: Mi hermana trabajó los últimos cuatro años para obtener su título. Para mí, gastar esa cantidad de dinero vale la pena.

Liz: Eso es muy amable de tu parte. Ojalá que nos estuviéramos graduando hoy. ¡Esto es muy emocionante!

Annie: Solo nos falta tres años y habremos terminado también. Nos graduaremos antes de darnos cuenta. El tiempo pasa muy rápido.

GRADUATION

Liz: That is a wonderful bouquet of flowers. Who is it for?

Annie: These flowers are for my sister Silvia. She is graduating today.

Liz: It must have cost you a fortune.

Annie: I paid seventy dollars for them.

Liz: That is quite expensive.

Annie: My sister worked very the last four years for her degree. To me spending that amount of money is worth it.

Liz: That is very nice of you. I wish we were graduating today. This is so exciting!

Annie: We only have another three years and we will be done also. We'll be graduating before we realize it. Time goes by very fast.

46. Noche de Brujas – Halloween

Eli: ¿Puedes creer que mañana es Halloween, Allison? ¡El tiempo pasa tan rápido! ¡Hoy es 30 de octubre! ¿Ya has decidido qué disfraz quieres usar?

Allison: Todavía estoy indecisa. Quiero usar un disfraz de tostadora o un disfraz de gángster de rap. Siempre me he preguntado por qué es una tradición vestirse para Halloween.

Eli: ¡Vestirse hace que celebrar las fiestas sea mucho más divertido!

Allison: Sí, recuerdo haberme divertido mucho el año pasado cuando mamá me llevó con un atuendo de gato. ¿Ya sabes lo que quieres ser, Eli?

Eli: ¡Quiero una ardilla!

Allison: ¡Es una gran idea!

Eli: ¡Genial! Entonces serás un rapero gángster y seré una ardilla. Vamos a preguntarle a mamá si podemos ir a pedir dulces mañana por la noche.

Allison: Ok, ¡Vamos a preguntarle a mamá!

HALLOWEEN

Eli: Can you believe that tomorrow is Halloween Allison? Time goes by so fast! Today is October 30th! Have you already decided what costume you want to wear?

Allison: I'm still undecided. I want to wear either a toaster costume or a gangster rapper costume. I have always wondered why it's a tradition to dress up for Halloween.

Eli: Dressing up makes celebrating the holiday much more fun!

Allison: Yes, I remember having a lot of fun last year when mom took me around in a cat outfit. Do you know what you want to be yet, Eli?

Eli: I want to a chipmunk!

Allison: That's a great idea!

Eli: Great! So you will be a gangster rapper and I will be a chipmunk. Let's go ask mom if we can go trick-or-treating tomorrow night by ourselves.

Allison: Ok, let's go ask mom!

47. EN UN HOTEL – AT A HOTEL

Recepcionista del hotel: Buenas noches.

Eli: Hola, buenas noches. Mi esposa y yo necesitamos una habitación para solo una noche, por favor. Por casualidad, ¿tiene una disponible?

Recepcionista del hotel: ¿Usted tiene una reserva?

Eli: Desafortunadamente, no tenemos una reserva.

Recepcionista del hotel: Ok. Déjame revisar y ver lo que tenemos. Parece que estás de suerte. Solo nos queda una habitación.

Eli: Excelente. Hemos estado conduciendo todo el día y estamos muy cansados. Solo necesitamos un lugar para descansar por el resto de la noche.

Recepcionista del hotel: Esta habitación debería estar bien entonces. Es una habitación acogedora con una cama tamaño grande y cocina completa.

Eli: ¿Cuánto se debe pagar por noche?

Recepcionista del hotel: Es $ 179 por la habitación. ¿Hay alguien más que se quede en la habitación con ustedes?

Eli: Somos solo nosotros dos. Sé que es tarde por la noche, pero ¿hay algún restaurante abierto cerca?

Recepcionista del hotel: Hay un restaurante abierto por una hora más en el hotel. ¿Quieres pagar la habitación con una tarjeta de crédito?

Eli: Sí. Aqui tiene.

Recepcionista del hotel: Gracias. Ya está listo. Disfruta el resto de la noche.

AT A HOTEL

Hotel Receptionist: Good evening.

Eli: Hello, good evening. My wife and I need a room for the night please. By chance do you have one available?

Hotel Receptionist: Do you have a reservation?

Eli: Unfortunately, we do not have a reservation.

Hotel Receptionist: Ok. Let me check and see what we have. It looks you're in luck. We have only one room left.

Eli: Excellent. We have been driving all day and we're very tired. We just need a place to relax for the rest of the night.

Hotel Receptionist: This room should do just fine then. It is a cozy room with a king size bed and full kitchen.

Eli: How much is it for the night?

Hotel Receptionist: It's $179 for the room. Is there anyone else staying in the room with you?

Eli: It's just the two of us. I know that it's late at night, but is there any restaurant open nearby?

Hotel Receptionist: There's a restaurant open for another hour in the hotel. Do you want to pay for the room with a credit card?

Eli: Yes. Here you go.

Hotel Receptionist: Thank you. You're all set. Enjoy the rest of the night.

48. Un Estudiante Extranjero – A Foreign Student

Drew: Hola, ¿es usted la señora McNamara?

Sra. McNamara: Sí, soy yo. Debes ser Drew. Te hemos estado esperando.

Drew: Se suponía que debía llegar hace dos días, pero mi vuelo de salida de Colombia se retrasó.

Sra. McNamara: Bueno, me alegro de que hayas llegado a salvo, eso es lo más importante. ¿Te gustaría un poco de té?

Drew: Me encantaría, si no le molesta. Tiene una hermosa casa.

Sra. McNamara: Gracias. Nos mudamos a California desde Colombia hace cinco años y decidimos comprar esta casa. Nos encanta.

Drew: Le traje un regalo.

Sra. McNamara: Oh, no debiste haberlo hecho. Este es un hermoso collar. Gracias. ¿Cuánto tiempo estarás aquí?

Drew: De nada. Planeo quedarme en California por cinco meses para practicar inglés. Estoy muy emocionado de ir a la escuela de inglés y aprender.

Sra. McNamara: Bueno, déjame mostrarte tu habitación y puedes relajarte. Debes estar cansado por viajar tanto.

A Foreign Student

Drew: Hello, are you Mrs. McNamara?

Mrs. McNamara: Yes, I am. You must be Drew. We have been expecting you.

Drew: I was supposed to arrive two days ago, but my flight out of Colombia was delayed.

Mrs. McNamara: Well, I'm glad that you made it safely, that's is what is most important. Would you like some tea?

Drew: I would love some, if it's not too much trouble. You have a beautiful home.

Mrs. McNamara: Thank you. We moved to California from Colombia five years ago and decided to buy this house. We absolutely love it.

Drew: I brought you a gift.

Mrs. McNamara: Oh, you shouldn't have. This is a beautiful necklace. Thank you. How long will you be here for?

Drew: You're welcome. I plan to stay in California for five months to practice speaking English. I am really excited to go to the English school and learn.

Mrs. McNamara: Well, let me show you your room and you can relax. You must be tired from all of the traveling.

49. Procrastinación – Procrastination

Scottie: ¿Ya has escrito tu informe? Tienes que entregarlo en dos semanas.

Meredith: No, todavía no he comenzado a trabajar en eso. Sin embargo, tendré mucho tiempo para hacerlo la próxima semana.

Scottie: Recuerdo claramente que eso es lo que dijiste la semana pasada y la semana anterior. Como tienes tanto tiempo libre durante las vacaciones, debes hacerlo.

Meredith: El problema es que no me va bien en esa clase y creo que podría necesitar un tutor. Sí no, podría fallar con toda esa clase.

Scottie: Tengo una solución. Deja de pensar en obtener ayuda y realmente consigue un tutor.

Meredith: Tienes razón. Necesito ser proactiva y obtener ayuda. Voy a buscar mañana.

Scottie: ¿Mañana? ¡No, tienes que encontrar uno hoy mismo!

Meredith: Lo sé, solo estoy bromeando. Lo haré hoy.

PROCRASTINATION

Scottie: Have you written your research report yet? It's due in two weeks.

Meredith: No, I haven't started working on it yet. I have plenty of time to do it next week though.

Scottie: I distinctly remember that's what you said last week and the week before that. Since you have so much free time during the holiday you should get it done.

Meredith: The problem is that I am struggling in that class and I think I might need to get a tutor. Otherwise I might fail the entire class.

Scottie: I have a solution. Stop thinking about getting help and get a tutor.

Meredith: You're right. I need to be proactive and get help. I start looking tomorrow.

Scottie: Tomorrow? No, you have to find one today!

Meredith: I know, I'm just kidding. I will do it today.

50. Dónde Está Mi Hermano – Where's My Brother

Carissa: No puedo encontrar a mi hermanito. Pensé que estaba justo detrás de mí y ahora está perdido. Por favor, ayúdeme.

Oficial de policía: Probablemente se perdió entre la multitud. Hay mucha gente comprando para las fiestas. ¿Qué tipo de ropa tiene puesta?

Carissa: Él tiene una chaqueta azul y pantalones cortos negros. Solo tiene 5 años.

Oficial de policía: Creo que lo vi entrar al camerino. Dejame revisar. ¿Tiene el pelo rubio?

Carissa: Sí, ¡¿lo encontraste?!

Oficial de policía: No, no era él. Revisemos la juguetería de al lado.

Carissa: ¡Le encanta jugar con Legos, yo debí haber pensado en eso!

Oficial de policía: Veo muchos niños en todas partes. ¿Alguno de ellos es tu hermano?

Carissa: ¡Daniel! Ahí estás, ¡No te vayas así de nuevo! ¡Me diste un susto de muerte!

Oficial de policía: Por favor, vigílelo para que esto no vuelva a ocurrir. Puede ser peligroso deambular solo.

Carissa: Tiene razón. Cuidaré mejor de mirarlo.

Oficial de policía: Bien. Ahora ve a buscar a tus padres y ten un buen día.

Carissa: Gracias señor por toda su ayuda.

WHERE'S MY BROTHER

Carissa: I can't find my little brother, Daniel. I thought he was right behind me and now he's missing. Please help me.

Police officer: He probably got lost in the crowd. There are a lot of people shopping for the holidays. What kind of clothes is he wearing?

Carissa: He has a blue jacket and black shorts. He's only 5 years old.

Police officer: I think I saw him go into the dressing room. Let me check. Does he have blonde hair?

Carissa: Yes. Did you find him?

Police officer: No, that was not him. Let's check the toy store next door.

Carissa: He loves playing with Legos, I should have thought of that!

Police officer: I see a lot of children everywhere. Are any of them your brother?

Carissa: Daniel! There you are, don't you wander off like that again! You scared me to death!

Police officer: Please keep an eye on him so that this doesn't happen again. It can be dangerous wandering around all by himself.

Carissa: You're right. I will take better care of watching him.

Police officer: Alright. Now go find your parents and have a good day.

Carissa: Thank you officer for all of your help.

Conclusion

Well reader, we hope that you found these dual language dialogues helpful. Remember the best way to learn this material is through repetition, memorization and conversation.

We encourage you to review the dialogues again, find a friend and practice your Spanish by role playing. Not only will you have more fun doing it this way, but you will find that you will remember even more!

Keep in mind, that every day you practice, the closer you will get to speaking fluently.

You can expect many more books from us, so keep your eyes peeled. Thank you again for reading our book and we look forward to seeing you again.

ABOUT THE AUTHOR

Touri is an innovative language education brand that is disrupting the way we learn languages. Touri has a mission to make sure language learning is not just easier but engaging and a ton of fun.

Besides the excellent books that they create, Touri also has an active website, which offers live fun and immersive 1-on-1 online language lessons with native instructors at nearly anytime of the day.

Additionally, Touri provides the best tips to improving your memory retention, confidence while speaking and fast track your progress on your journey to fluency.

Check out https://touri.co for more information.

OTHER BOOKS BY TOURI

SPANISH

Spanish Short Stories (Volume 1): 10 Exciting Short Stories to Easily Learn Spanish & Improve Your Vocabulary

Spanish Short Stories (Volume 2): 10 Exciting Short Stories to Easily Learn Spanish & Improve Your Vocabulary

Intermediate Spanish Short Stories (Volume 1): 10 Amazing Short Tales to Learn Spanish & Quickly Grow Your Vocabulary the Fun Way!

Intermediate Spanish Short Stories (Volume 2): 10 Amazing Short Tales to Learn Spanish & Quickly Grow Your Vocabulary the Fun Way!

100 Days of Real World Spanish: Useful Words & Phrases for All Levels to Help You Become Fluent Faster

100 Day Medical Spanish Challenge: Daily List of Relevant Medical Spanish Words & Phrases to Help You Become Fluent

FRENCH

Conversational French Dialogues: 50 French Conversations and Short Stories

French Short Stories for Beginners (Volume 1): 10 Exciting Short Stories to Easily Learn French & Improve Your Vocabulary

French Short Stories for Beginners (Volume 2): 10 Exciting Short Stories to Easily Learn French & Improve Your Vocabulary

ITALIAN

Conversational Italian Dialogues: 50 Italian Conversations and Short Stories

One Last Thing...

If you enjoyed this book or found it useful, we would be very grateful if you posted a short review on Amazon.

Your support really does make a difference and we read all the reviews personally. Your feedback will make this book even better.

Thanks again for your support!

FREE SPANISH VIDEO COURSE

200+ words and phrases in audio

you can start using today!

Get it while it's available

https://touri.co/freespanishvideocourse-spanish-dialogues/

Lightning Source UK Ltd.
Milton Keynes UK
UKHW021113161021
392321UK00011B/235

9 781953 149190